Avoid the Five Biggest Mistakes In Estate Planning

And Save Thousands of Dollars in Legal Fees, Probate and Taxes

An easy to understand guide to the principles of estate planning and how to protect yourself from the traps and dangers.

Richard A. Behlmann

Avoid the Five Biggest Mistakes in Estate Planning,

And Save Thousands of Dollars in Legal Fees, Probate and Taxes

Richard A. Behlmann
Behlmann Law Firm, LP
21218 Kingsland Blvd
Katy, TX 77450
Copyright ©2007 Richard Behlmann

Published by:
      Gateway Media Services
      Houston, Texas

Introduction

This book is intended to cover the essential steps needed to create an estate plan and the dangers to avoid in clear and understandable terms. It also explains to the lucky ones with large and complex estates, that strategies exist to save them big bucks in taxes and avoid a lot of hassle down the road.

This book is dedicated to my brother, Steve, and folks like him with estates worth planning for who passed away before their time. Having had both a brother and a brother-in-law who died at a young age I know the unexpected can happen to anyone. Fortunately, they each had a plan in place and things went smoothly, but many do not have lawyers in the family, so we put together this guide to walk you through it.

Those who need this information most -- have the least free time and need it straight and simple. So we designed it to be read in a single afternoon or a short airline flight. If you see the problems as too complex you won't take the simple steps to solve it.

So for all of you who know you should do something but didn't know what to do, this book is for you. Taking charge of your life was never simpler.

Richard Behlmann

Table of Contents

Special Sections:

"Do not take life too seriously.
You will never get out alive."
~~*Elbert Hubbard*

Chapter 1 – Estate Planning the Basics

In my 30 years of dealing with clients I find there is a great deal of confusion on the topic of estate planning. In some cases this is intentional -- used to create client anxiety resulting in an increase in fees and purchases of financial products.

To be fair it is a complex area encompassing many facets of the law and a high level of emotion. Many people get confused over some very difficult topics. "Estate planning" is a service sold in one form or another by insurance agents, financial planners, accountants and attorneys, each with its own perspective and products to sell.

This book is based on a philosophy that anyone can plan their own estate once they understand their options. By presenting your options in a simple understandable format and using case examples, you will be able to make the decisions central to having a plan that achieves your goals in the most cost effective manner.

Let's start with the basics. What is estate planning? Estate planning is simply the process of looking at what assets and property you own and deciding how you would like those things handled in the event you died or became incapable of managing your own affairs.

The simplest plan is of course to spend everything while you are alive. That way there is no concern about how or who will dispose of your assets after your passing. Unfortunately, to do this successfully requires incredible timing and conflicts with most people's other great fear -- outliving their money. In fact, a recent survey indicates retirees number one fear is outliving their money. Hence, the need for some formal plan for your own peace of mind.

Assuming you're not willing to bet it all on perfect timing your planning options are going to be based on the types and amount of assets you hold and the control you wish to exercise from the grave.

The most effective estate plan for you could be anything from a simple change in some beneficiary forms to complex trusts and wills designed to save taxes and protect and manage your assets for the next hundred years.

As we go through the issues you will gain the knowledge to decide which end of the spectrum is most effective for you.

Regardless of the size of your estate, there are four steps to creating your plan.

1.   Know What You Have in Estate

First, you need to take an inventory of everything you have, including anything that may be coming to you in the future and any current or future debts you may incur over the remaining years of your life. This may include an expected future inheritance, life insurance benefits or other long term but predictable occurrences.

2.   Decide How You Want It Distributed

Secondly, you will need to make some decisions regarding what you want to happen with that property. What would happen to it if you were disabled and ultimately what would you like to happen to your assets upon your death.

3. Decide Who You Want to Handle Your Property & Your Medical Decisions

People decisions are the next choice. There are several "jobs" in an estate plan. You will have to identify one or more people in addition to your wife or husband to manage your affairs. You will need a person or persons you trust because you will be giving them a great deal of power.

You will be giving two different kinds of power. The official term is appointing a power of attorney. One is a power of attorney for property and the other is a power of attorney for healthcare.

The property power deals with the distribution and management of your property. This includes your final bills, details, taxes, insurance, etc. The person you appoint may need some administrative skills or at least not be afraid of balancing checkbooks, dealing with taxes, etc. The more complex your assets the more help they may need.

While administrative skills are valuable, confidence in their ability to handle your affairs is really more important than specific skills. A trusted friend or family member can always hire accountants or other professionals to help in the event you were disabled or passed away.

The healthcare power relates to medical decisions. Your healthcare or medical power of attorney is the person that would make your healthcare decisions if you could not. In most cases this does not involve some extreme form of personal illness but can be used for more temporary or emergency-type care. For example, you are unconscious from an accident or more commonly you are in surgery and temporarily under anesthetic due to an operation. When this happens the doctors will want to know who they should talk to about treatment decisions, because you cannot make your own choices.

The person you choose as your healthcare decision-maker does not have to be the same person you put in charge of your assets. For example, if your spouse was not available or you were unmarried, you might want your mother or brother to handle the healthcare decisions, even though you would never let them manage your property. It is an important responsibility and some people may be uncomfortable with that kind of responsibility.

4. Create the Documents or Changes That Will Follow Your Wishes

Once you have made your choices on number one, two and three the last step is determining and putting in place the correct legal documents and beneficiary forms required to appoint the people you chose and allow them to do their job.

As you can see breaking down things task by task, that none of these decisions is beyond the abilities of the average person. However, most people never take the time to stop and think through what would happen if they were not there.

You may have a plan in mind and think everyone knows what you want but never write it down or discuss it with anyone. Unless written down it remains just a thought, which unfortunately will pass away with you on your death.

Fortunately or unfortunately depending on your point of view, your state has a plan for those who don't get around to creating their own. The state or probate court will take the same steps as we discussed above.

However, without you in the picture, the probate courts, your heirs and their lawyers, moving with government-like efficiency will make and argue those decisions through the court system. In the end they will spend a lot more of your money and may give your estate to someone you didn't intend. It is even more interesting if you have minor children.

Another complication is property in multiple states. Because no single state has authority to direct how property is disposed of in another state. It will require the probate court of each state to get involved and make decisions regarding property within its borders.

As you can see, even people who feel their estate may not be very large may have expensive complexities by owning property such as, vacation condos in Florida or Colorado, fishing camps in Louisiana, beach houses in Texas or just a clubhouse along the river somewhere. There are many options for dealing with this type of situation, some simple and some more complex. However, regardless of the plan, having any plan will be simpler and less complex ultimately than not having one.

Before we get started let's cover a few other points for clarity to keep everyone on the same page.

First, the term "estate". Your estate is everything you own or have some rights to. For example, if you have a partial interest in property your grandfather left you, that would be included as part of your estate.

The obvious ones are your home and other real estate, bank accounts and investment accounts, those areas everybody assumes are part of your estate. But your estate also includes personal effects such as jewelry or collections. Often these items can cause the most trouble because of their sentimental value. I knew a family that didn't speak for twelve years because someone took a watch and chain others thought they were not entitled to.

Larger items of personal property such as cars, trucks, boats, RVs, and farm equipment usually have a title or other document that controls their ownership. Having these ownership documents made out incorrectly can create difficulty for your heirs in managing this property once you are gone.

Your estate also includes life insurance, retirement accounts, annuities, promissory notes for money you loaned to your cousin or brother-in-law and claims against people you may have provided services or goods to who never paid you. All of these things are included in your estate.

The "estate" we have discussed above is everything you own. You would use this "estate" to determine if you had to pay estate taxes.

Planning Point: Property can be included in your taxable estate even if it is transferred on your death to another person. For example life insurance you own will be paid to your named beneficiary but will be included in your taxable estate for estate tax purposes.

Estate taxes are determined by the IRS and the rules are uniform from state to state. That being said and without the intent to confuse you further in certain areas, the IRS may rely on your state's laws for certain interpretations. But for the most part estate taxes are governed by the IRS rules.

Your "probate estate" is actually something different and may not cover the same assets. We'll discuss these differences later in the book so for the moment just be aware that different types of "estates" exist and depending on which one someone is talking about different things can occur.

Planning Point: Probate is a state court process. Each state has its own unique rules and requirements for getting through it.

One practical tip is to make it so those surviving you can find your property. Life insurance policies, stock certificates or other items hidden away for safety or a rainy day may remain hidden after you are gone, lost forever.

With these basics on what an estate is and what estate planning does, let's jump in cover the mistakes, which can thousands in unnecessary expenses and sometimes even more important time and aggravation.

*What a wonderful life I've had! I only
wish I'd realized it sooner. ~~Unknown*

Chapter 2 - There Are Worse Things Than Death

*Mistake Number One: Failing to Plan for
Incapacity "Living Probate"*

Most people are familiar with the fact
they should have a will. They have a vague
understanding about how wills work. They've
seen them in the movies where rich people
torture their relatives beyond the grave by
creating exotic clauses and unusual conditions
in order to get the money they've always
wanted. People realize a lot of this is
Hollywood spin and not everyone is Brewster's
Millions or any of the other dozen films dealing
with peculiarities in grandpa's will.

However, deep down you know you
should have one and you know putting it off is
ultimately going to cost you one way or another.

Sometimes the need for peace of mind
becomes motivation enough for you to create a
will, even if it is only downloading a form from

the Internet, filling in the blanks and having a friend or two witness it.

People think about wills and know death is inevitable but do not consider situations where they sustain serious injuries such as a stroke or car accidents or more progressive debilitating diseases such as Alzheimer's and Parkinson's.

Planning for incapacity can be very simple and is really the area where you are doing something for yourself while you are alive, not your heirs.

I consider it the most important part of your plan. Here is my logic. If you die, you are dead and pretty much out of the picture. Ultimately if you failed to plan it really becomes someone else's problem. But if you are incapacitated and others can not take care of you it affects you while you are alive. It also means they will be using up your money in needless legal and administrative fees to take care of you.

The key is to make sure that in the event you are incapacitated or are temporarily unable to manage your own affairs you have a backup plan which can be put in place before your assets are completely decimated.

We live in a world where medical miracles have the potential to keep someone alive in a disabled condition for a very long time. Knowing this, people still do not think about the fact that a debilitating stroke, head injury or other condition would be more devastating to their financial and personal condition than actually passing away. This is why I consider this the most critical area of planning.

There are two issues when you are incapacitated. One is handling your property and the second is handling your medical and healthcare needs.

These are handled by separate documents. The two major ways property and finances can be handled is by providing a "durable" power of attorney and/or a revocable living trust. The durable power of attorney for property or a revocable living trust do not give a person any rights to deal with healthcare decisions.

To manage your healthcare decisions if you are incapacitated you will need a medical or healthcare power of attorney. A healthcare power of attorney only covers medical issues and does not grant any rights or create any powers for that person to deal with your property or finances.

Having appropriate medical and property documents in place is a simple process. As with most estate planning issues, the solution is simple and without a plan the risk is great and expensive.

Here is an all too common example, you have an unexpected stroke or heart attack and can no longer take care of yourself. Your money is frozen. Your friends or family can't go down to your bank or broker and draw out money to take care of you. Without a living trust or powers of attorney your assets and investment choices will be frozen until someone is appointed your legal guardian.

Someone will have to apply for a guardianship or conservatorship on your behalf and manage your affairs with the "help" of the court. That person may or may not be the person you would have chosen. Worse than that is having several of your relatives fighting over who gets to be appointed with your money.

This process is "living probate" and you have officially lost control of your life. Guardianship is a state court process usually handled by the same courts that handle probate matters and each state is a little different. Although the process is different the steps are similar.

1. You are officially declared incompetent in a public court proceeding.

2. The court appoints at least one extra lawyer, an ad litem, to protect your interest. (This in addition to the lawyer your family has hired to apply for the guardianship. You pay for both)

3. The court takes away your power to manage your own affairs and appoints someone to take care of you.

4. The court requires regular reports, a bond and other reporting, all of which your estate gets to pay for.

If all of this sounds expensive, it is. To me guardianship can be one of the most expensive processes in terms of money and emotions someone can go through in the legal system. Primarily, because it can be avoided so easily.

Planning Point: In some cases guardianships are unavoidable and serve a necessary purpose. For example, there are no alternatives in providing for the needs of a disabled or handicapped child who becomes an adult.

Guardianship is a court process designed solely to protect the incapacitated person. Once you are incapacitated by a stroke or injury you can no longer protect yourself and the court has a number of safeguards to prevent someone from wrongly obtaining control of your assets.

First, the guardianship application is heard in open court, a public process. A hearing is set, you are brought into the courtroom and openly declared incompetent. The court then hears evidence of the extent of your affairs and the need for a guardian. It then reviews the list of eligible persons and based on the findings and evidence makes its selection. This may or not be the person you would have chosen.

Remember you are now incapacitated and the court doesn't know whether your representative has your best interests at heart or is merely a relative trying to make a power grab to put grandpa away and gain control of your money. The court also has many other cases and so it will hire someone, another lawyer to check out the situation. The second lawyer is of course at your expense since it is for your benefit.

This second lawyer is known as an ad litem. The ad litem is "your lawyer" he or she represents your interests as the incapacitated person.

The ad litem's job is to investigate your condition, evaluate your estate and recommend the appropriate person to manage your affairs.

If you would have made a plan you may have wanted your husband, wife or eldest child to take over the management of your affairs. Once the ad litem and the judge get involved they may decide your estate is too complex or your husband or wife is not in good enough physical condition to take on the responsibility. The ad litem is liable if he or she is not thorough or adequately protecting you. Therefore, if you have significant financial assets the ad litem may determine that someone else or a professional trustee should really manage your property.

At the end of the investigation the ad litem prepares a report which is provided to the court. Based on the ad litem's report and the evidence provided by the person applying for your guardianship the court decides who will manage your personal and financial affairs.

Once the court has selected your guardian, this person remains under the supervision of the court, even if it is your wife or husband. They are required on an ongoing basis to report back to the court with various accountings and inventories regarding what they are doing with your money.

Even if the court appoints the person you would have selected they are still required to go through the process and incur the expense, appointing the ad litem and making their annual accountings and reports. And of course, all of this activity is paid for by you out of your assets. In a small estate this administration could eat up a large percentage. The tragedy is it could have been avoided by having a simple plan in place.

Fred Sanford: Didn't you learn anything from being my son? Who do you think I am doing all this for?

Lamont Sanford: Yourself.

Fred Sanford: Yeah, you learned something.

Chapter 3 - Protection Against Contingencies Legal Documents & Alternatives

To avoid your assets and your estate plan from being hijacked, part of your estate plan needs to provide for the management of your property and the handling of your medical decisions in the event you are disabled or incapacitated.

At a minimum you need your state's version of a durable power of attorney in place in case you are incapacitated.

There are other alternatives discussed below such as revocable living trusts which are more flexible and may work better depending on your situation.

Your estate plan also needs a power of attorney for healthcare. This document appoints someone as your agent to make your healthcare decisions in the event of incapacity.

It should also include a living will or directive to physicians. This is the document where you tell your family what you want if your condition becomes terminal or you go into a permanent vegetative state. If you let them know what you would have wanted it removes the burden of this critical decision from your loved ones. Your healthcare options and alternatives are discussed in more detail below.

I. The Property Documents

A. Property Power-Of-Attorney

A power of attorney appoints another person as your agent. They do not need to be a lawyer, but can be any person you choose. The power of attorney enables your agent to sign your name with the same authority you have. If you are using a power of attorney for estate planning you want to make sure it is a "Durable Power of Attorney".

Unless specifically authorized by state law, as durable, a power of attorney becomes ineffective when a person is incapacitated.

This was based on the legal principle that you cannot grant rights you do not have. If you are disabled you do not have the capacity to sign for yourself, therefore, if you could not sign for yourself, you could not authorize someone else to sign on your behalf.

Before durable power of attorney laws were put into place a power of attorney became invalid when the person giving the power became incapacitated. All states now allow you to create a "durable" power of attorney which is specifically allowed to exist after the person who granted it becomes disabled.

Planning Point: A durable power of attorney does not extend beyond the person's life. If a person passes away all powers of attorney become void at that time.

Having a valid durable power of attorney for property is an essential part of a good estate plan. Typically husbands and wives appoint each other as their power-of-attorney but that is not required. To be on the safe side a person should appoint at least two alternates in case your first choice is either unavailable or perhaps injured in the same accident.

You can appoint anyone as your agent under a power of attorney. People often appoint their children, a brother or sister or even a parent to fill that role, but it can be a friend or even a professional like a CPA or lawyer. These can be set up to only take effect if a person is disabled, therefore, no powers are granted at the initial signing and if there is never a disability they are never used.

One caution here is that even though a power of attorney is properly executed and legally valid, the institution you are presenting it to may choose not to accept it. The institution is liable in the event they distribute funds on an invalid or revoked power of attorney.

Because they can not validate whether or not you revoked or cancelled the power of attorney, they will err on the side of caution. They may not accept a power of attorney over two or three years old or might only accept their own form executed in their offices.

If you look at it from their standpoint, a person they have never seen comes into their offices, presents a five year old power of attorney and wants to become a signer on an account or worse, wants to transfer all of their customer's money to a new account. And, because you are incapacitated the bank has no way to verify whether you did or did not appoint this person.

One thing you can do is to speak with your bank ahead of time to make sure they know you have appointed someone and who it is. That way several years from now if your brother comes in from out of town and tries to use your power of attorney they may at least have a note in the file or they may give you their own document to execute ahead of time.

If you have significant assets in an institution you may want to check on their policy or use their own form. Also bear in mind that with the mergers of banks and brokerage firms their policy today may become someone else's policy tomorrow when you need to use it.

B. The Revocable Living Trust

Grantor trusts are an estate planning workhorse that when used properly can save taxes, avoid probate and create asset protection. A grantor trust is a trust you set up for yourself as grantor, trustee and beneficiary. What other limitations and powers you create are based on what you are trying to accomplish.

The most common grantor trust is the revocable living trust which is used while you are alive to hold title to your assets avoiding probate on death and avoiding a guardianship while you are alive.

As part of setting it up you actually transfer the title to your property to the name of the trust. You are your own grantor , (Also called a trustor or settlor) trustee and beneficiary. The trust can be revoked or amended and assets can be added or removed at any time. The living trust now "owns" your assets. The legal reason this trust is effective as an estate planning device is that a trust doesn't die or get sick, only the trustees, beneficiaries or creators can have problems. The living trust is a contract you make with yourself and its terms provides the options of what to do with your property if something happens to you. In other words you can use one document to cover all of your property and define what happens.

For example, if you have real estate or other property in different states, lots of different assets or accounts, a family business or other items, you can control them all by the living trust. If something changes you can change the disposition of all the assets by changing your living trust. The difference between this and a will is it doesn't take a court to authorize the changes or distributions. It all happens privately and more importantly without delay or additional cost.

Another major benefit of a revocable trust is if something happens to you and you become incapacitated, the trust continues and whoever you appointed as your successor trustee takes over immediately without interruption and can use your assets to take care of you. This is something a will can never do because it only becomes effective if you die.

Your living trust would work like this. Let's say you are in a car accident and end up unconscious or in a coma and are laid up in the hospital. Your successor trustee as named in the trust would go down to the bank or other institution, present a physician's certificate and their identification and would be able to immediately step in and manage your affairs and get your bills paid etc. while you are out of commission. Assuming you were disabled for an extended period or permanently, the Trustee would stay in place and have the power to continue to manage your assets, for example, selling your three story townhouse and purchasing a more wheelchair friendly ranch style home or temporarily setting you up in an assisted living facility or provide other rehabilitation.

If you regain your capacity you would automatically take back control of your affairs. We will discuss this more in a later section of the book but if you never recover and eventually pass away the revocable living trust will also direct the disposition of your assets on your death, avoiding probate and the involvement of the courts.

You might think this sounds a lot like the power of attorney for property. The key difference between the Revocable Living Trust and the power of attorney is your agent under a power of attorney is acting on your account under delegated authority. The bank or broker can choose not to honor the appointment of your agent and it does not have the ability to verify that you actually gave this person the authority and whether it is still valid. If the bank allows your agent to make changes to your account or withdraw funds and the power of attorney had been revoked or withdrawn the bank is liable.

Under your revocable trust your successor trustee is named in the Trust document as the successor, the trust is the owner of the account and the Trustee is taking over the account as Trustee, not an agent. The bank can be forced to accept the successor trustee under the terms of your trust. If you failed to notify the bank or broker regarding a change you made in the Trust document they are not liable because they are following the terms of the trust. Your successor trustee is also under a fiduciary duty to follow the terms of the trust and protect your assets, an agent under your power of attorney is not governed by the same restrictions.

The revocable living trust is a very versatile instrument and can provide benefits both during your life and after your death.

There are many other types of trusts that can be used in your estate plan to accomplish other specific planning goals. The use of these trusts can be beneficial under the proper circumstances.

Trusts are used to control your assets on your behalf when you can no longer manage them either because of death or disability. If you desire to exercise control beyond the grave some of these more specialized trusts could be beneficial.

Some patients though conscious that their condition is perilous, recover their health simply through their contentment with the goodness of the physician.

~~~ Hippocrates 460 – 400 B.C.

II. The Healthcare Documents

A. Power of Attorney for Healthcare

The power of attorney for healthcare is authorized by specific statutes in each state. Because of this each state will have a slight variation in what they require in order to make the form valid.

This document is similar to the property power-of-attorney, except it deals with healthcare issues not property issues. The healthcare power of attorney is designed to take effect if the person is incapacitated.

It can be used in a number of situations which have nothing to do with dementia or permanent incapacity. For example, you are having surgery and are under anesthesia. You are incapacitated and unavailable. If the doctors encounter something during surgery and they need a treatment decision they can't bring you out of the anesthesia to ask. They will look to the person you appointed as your healthcare power of attorney. In other cases you may be in a coma following an accident or stroke and need someone to make your decisions for you for extended periods of time.

Regardless of the severity or the length of your injury the power of attorney for healthcare assumes that it is a temporary document and then at some point you will regain control of your own medical decisions. Once again it is recommended that a person appoint at least two alternates in case for example, you have appointed your spouse and you are both injured in the same accident.

Healthcare powers of attorney are defined by state law and their provisions will vary from state to state. You will need to have documents that meet the terms defined by your state of residence.

B. The Living Will, also known as, Directive to Physicians

The living will or directive to physicians is a document that comes into play if you end up incapacitated and in a terminal condition or an irreversible vegetative state. It is where you express your desires at the end of your life.

Your living will indicates whether or not you want the medical community to use extraneous measures, experimental surgeries and machines, such as a ventilator to keep you alive or you would like to be kept comfortable and pass away under your own terms.

These documents are authorized specifically by state statute and therefore each state has their own variation of what is required to make them effective. The individual states also vary the terms and the elections you make under these types of documents. Some are a simple one page and others are multi-page instruments where you can be more specific regarding what treatments you will or will not agree to.

C. How your Healthcare Documents Work Together

It helps to understand how the healthcare documents work together. That way you will know who is making the decisions at different points in time.

As you pass through or incur certain conditions they work roughly like this.

Stage One: Healthy and competent.

You make your own medical decisions as long as you are able.

Stage Two: You are not terminal but are temporarily or permanently incapacitated.

Your healthcare power of attorney determines who makes your healthcare decisions. One thing to bear in mind is that the healthcare power of attorney assumes you will someday regain the ability to make your own decisions.

It could also be used in situations such as, you are in surgery and the doctors need a treatment decision on an unexpected complication. They will look for the holder of your healthcare power of attorney to make that decision.

Stage Three: **Incapacitated and in a terminal or permanent vegetative state.**

If your condition continues to deteriorate and you end up with a terminal condition, (usually defined as less than six months to live and no treatment is available) or in a permanent vegetative state, then the power shifts away from your agent under the healthcare power of attorney and back to you.

Your Living Will or Directive to Physician controls, because you made this decision yourself as evidenced by a document you signed in front of witnesses at a time when you were not incapacitated.

The living will is intended to override the decisions of your agent under the healthcare power of attorney. This means that if your agent wanted to keep you alive at any cost and that was not your desire, your wishes would be followed. Similarly, if your agent wanted to take you off of life support, and you had stated you did not want that, their decision would not be followed.

For your own protection however, the living will is revocable verbally by you at anytime. So should you change your mind, the decision is not set in stone. And of course if you are not incapacitated you will make the decision yourself in person.

Because of the serious nature of this decision the terms which relate to your medical condition are defined in the statute.

There is a requirement that a medical professional, typically more than one, make a determination that either the person has a terminal illness or is in an irreversible permanent vegetative state without hope of recovery. Once these medical determinations have been made the decision of whether to remove machines keeping someone alive can be based on your directions under a living will.

The critical point here is that the living will allows you to make the decision. Just as importantly it removes the burden of the decision and any arguments regarding what you really wanted from your loved ones.

In my experience the choices under a living will can be very difficult. Clients get concerned because no one knows what the future will bring and they don't know who will be making the medical determination. The benefit to your family is you made the choice yourself so they know they are following your wishes.

Remember this is a very emotional time and the more you can provide a roadmap for those you love, the easier it will be on them and you.

D.   The Out of Hospital DNR

In some states an additional document referred to as a DNR or do not resuscitate request is also available and can be provided to emergency medical professionals, such as ambulance and EMS technicians preventing them from providing life-sustaining care.

Typically the DNR's referred to in this paragraph are put in place by people who have an existing condition already diagnosed and who are certain how they would like to be treated in the event of a medical emergency.

E. The HIPAA Release

The HIPAA release is based on a federal statute dealing with medical privacy laws. This document does not grant any decision-making power but does allow those people that you feel are appropriate to have open discussions with your medical professionals and to have access to your medical information. For example, if you listed your children or perhaps your brother or sister on your form they would be able to have a discussion with the physician regarding your condition. Without this type of instrument in place hospitals and physicians in an emergency would not be able to keep you informed.

This release is essential for anyone with your medical power of attorney. You would not want them in the position where they have to make decisions without having any access to your medical information.

While this sounds highly improbable and unlikely in an emergency situation where time is of the essence, you don't want hospital administration and the physicians trying to sort out privacy issues while you are trying to get treatment accomplished and inform your family regarding what is going on.

Another area where people don't always realize this kind of document can be helpful is in the case of adult children. Once your child reaches the age of 18, they are an adult and entitled to the same rights of medical privacy as everyone else. The fact that you are still paying for them and doing everything that you've been doing for the last 18 years does not automatically qualify you to get this information. Therefore, in the case of a college student this kind of document can help parents, and or whoever is making those decisions speed up the process in the event of an emergency.

If you don't know you don't know,
Then you think you know.

~~~ *Larry Freeman, Criminal*
Investigator

Chapter 4 – Understand the Difference Between Probate and Non-probate Assets

Mistake Number Two: Not Knowing How Your Assets Are Really Transferred.

To make sure your plan will work the way you want it to you need to understand how all your assets transfer. They can pass in a number of different ways.

I.   Non-Probate Transfers

A.   Beneficiaries and Pay on Death Designations

Some assets, such as life insurance or IRA's, transfer based on a beneficiary designation. Some accounts or property transfer based on a "POD" or "pay on death" designation. This works similar to a beneficiary form and will pay over the money or property to your designated

POD beneficiary on your death. For example, a bank account or CD with a pay on death designation will automatically transfer to the person you listed as your POD beneficiary.

For assets that transfer under beneficiary forms you need to make sure the designated beneficiary is the person you still want to receive the money.

B. Joint Tenants with Rights of Survivorship

Another type of automatic transfer is holding property as joint tenants with rights of survivorship. If you hold property as joint tenants with rights of survivorship on your death, the asset will automatically pass to the other joint tenant.

Planning Point: There can be some problems with joint tenancy because it makes someone a co-owner of your property. Also if the wrong joint tenant dies first, such as a child dying before their parent the property will flow back to the surviving joint tenant.

C. Property Held in a Revocable or Irrevocable Trust

Property held in a revocable trust transfers on your death outside of probate. In a revocable trust you have already transferred the property from yourself individually to your trust.

Upon your death, disability or whatever other event you specify, the terms of the trust work like a very sophisticated beneficiary form. When that event occurs, it lays out what will happen to all of the assets in the trust. For example, it might say that on your death take ½ of your estate and set up a trust for your disabled daughter and have the funds managed by her older sister. The trust allows you to exercise control beyond the grave passing the property to your beneficiary.

If you have a significant amount of assets or have concerns about how your beneficiary might manage the property or protect themselves from their own inexperience, trusts can be used to give you the peace of mind to know your family member will be taken care of.

D. Probate Assets

If you have not provided for or used one of the means above to facilitate the transfer of your assets, you will need the probate court to make the transfer for you. The probate court is the official means for transferring the title to your assets when they do not transfer another way.

For example, your aunt Jane passes away. She does not have any children and you are her only living relative so you figure the house will become yours. Before she died, she owned her home jointly with her husband who passed away several years before. The title to Aunt Jane's house was in her and her husband's name as joint tenants with right of survivorship, but both of them are now deceased. When her husband died several years ago the home automatically passed to her as the surviving joint tenant and she continued to live there without any problems.

Now that she has passed away, can you just move in and take over, sell the property to the highest bidder and keep the money? If not you, who does own the property? Even more basic, who would have the authority to list the property with a real estate agent? This is a probate asset because it needs some official action to transfer it to the next owner. Without some kind of official paperwork you have no more rights to it than anyone else.

The probate court is the official government body that will make the determination and issue the future owner a court order or other document that can be recorded in the deed records and give the new owner clear title. The probate court reaches its decision is one of two ways.

Option one, if Aunt Jane died with a will, her executor will initiate a probate proceeding and file the will with the court. The court will make sure Aunt Jane's will is valid and properly signed. If so it will follow Aunt Jane's wishes and authorize the transfer of the property to the person or person's designated by the will. Once authorized, her executor then processes the transfer and distributes the property to the appropriate person or organization. Unfortunately, for you, you discover Aunt Jane willed her house to her hairdresser and left you nothing. The will determines the distribution and being her closest relative does not automatically make you a beneficiary.

Option two, if Aunt Jane died without a will, her next of kin, as her potential heirs will apply for an heirship based on the inheritance laws of the state she died in. In other words your state of residence has written a will for everyone who dies without having written their own. It may not be what you would have wanted, and it will be more expensive and cumbersome to probate, but it will, no pun intended, transfer the property to the heirs, eventually.

Assets like this that require the intervention of the probate court in order to change the title are probate assets. It may be a house or other real estate, it could also be a bank or brokerage account that was only in your aunt's name at her death. The banks will also need some official paperwork to allow you or the beneficiary under the will to withdraw or reinvest the funds.

So probate assets are those that at the time of your death are only in your name or the name of someone who is deceased. They will have to go through the probate court so the court can officially authorize the change in title and get your assets to the right people. No one else has the authority to make these kinds of decisions.

Unless you have taken steps to facilitate the transfer on your death through some other means, a probate will be required to get your property to the right person.

Planning Point: Probate is also a means of resolving your final debts. Your probate assets get collected into your estate and your creditors make claims against them. Once everyone is paid the remainder goes to your heirs.

Non-probate assets such as life insurance pass to beneficiaries outside of probate. If your probate beneficiaries and insurance beneficiaries are not the same your probate beneficiaries could have their value reduced by paying all of the final debts.

Understanding how your assets will transfer is essential in getting your property to the right people. Your probate assets are controlled by your will or intestacy laws. Non probate assets are controlled by beneficiary forms and trust documents. Here are some additional examples where probate would be required or where you may have thought your will covered certain things and it did not.

1. You have received a stock certificate for 100 shares of Exxon from your grandfather when you graduated from college 30+ years ago. You were not married so the certificate is in your name only. You have been collecting dividends and holding on to the certificate as a reserve in case you ever needed it, never depositing it in a brokerage account. It is in a file somewhere and you look at it from time to time reminiscing about your grandfather's generosity.

After your death your children find the stock certificate and want to sell it and distribute the money. They take it to their broker and she says she can sell it, but she needs your executor to provide testamentary letters authorizing the transfer to your estate.

Because the stock certificate is only in your name, someone has to make an official determination who gets the money. Your broker will not make that decision but will rely on the probate courts to tell them who they should give it to.

2. You and your spouse are killed in a car wreck. Your children want to sell your house,

which was in both your names. When you die your children will not be able to just list your house with a real estate broker and then sign over a deed in your name once a buyer is found.

In order to sell your house and provide a clear title so the buyer can get title insurance and a mortgage, the house will have to pass through probate.

The sale proceeds will then be paid into your estate. The money will be reduced by any debts of your estate and the executor at some point will be able to distribute the money to the children.

As a rule of thumb, assets which you own at the time of your death only in your name are probate assets. These would pass under your will or heirship laws and require some form of probate to change the title.

3. You had a bank account and designated that on your death it should be paid to your daughter, Lucy Brown. Lucy Brown presents your death certificate to the bank and they pay over the money to her and close your account. By having a pay on death designation or a

beneficiary, this asset does not need probate to transfer its title and is no longer a probate asset.

It is important to understand how your assets are going to transfer so that when you are developing a plan you are aware of what's covered by your will and what will transfer automatically. You also need to understand the risks that exist in some pay on death and joint tenant transfers.

To illustrate the risks let's use some examples based on real life situations I have seen.

Case 1: You are unmarried and have three adult children. You have a $100,000 CD in the bank with a pay on death ("POD") designation for your three children. You also have your oldest daughter as a joint tenant/signer on your $350,000 brokerage account because she lives near you and just in case something happens to you she can help out. You rent your apartment and lease your car and do not own any other real estate or significant personal assets.

You know you have $450,000 in cash and stocks which you want shared by your three children equally. Your will says split it three ways equally so you think everything is taken care of. Not understanding your will does not affect nonprobate transfers, you believe the $450,000 will pass through your estate and be divided $ 150,000 to each of your three children.

On your death the $100,000 CD will be split three ways, $33,333 each. However, your oldest daughter as your surviving joint tenant will take over your $350,000 brokerage account. Your oldest daughter now has $383,333 and your other two children have $33,333 each. Your will won't even need to be probated because there are no assets left to be transferred.

Your oldest daughter has the power to keep all the money, or if her heart is in the right place, she can try and equalize your property among the three siblings.

The difficulty is transfers of this size are considered taxable gifts by the Internal Revenue Service. Therefore, she will be impacting her own estate planning by trying to give money to her brother and sister.

In a worst-case scenario she keeps all the brokerage account money and there is nothing anyone can do about it.

Case 2: Let's assume you have spoken with some friends and they have advised you of the danger of the strategy you have selected. You decide to fix this by making all of your children joint tenants with you on both the CD and the brokerage account. That way if something happens to you they will all share equally and everything will be taken care of.

Everything is going along smoothly until your youngest daughter finally decides to divorce the bum she married, as they are putting together the inventory of her assets for the divorce the "bum" or the bum's attorney tells her that she needs to list those assets where she is a joint tenant, i.e. your bank account and your brokerage account.

Now your assets are tied up in her divorce. And while ultimately you may be able to explain away the fact these are not really her assets, you have caused yourself unnecessary hassle and put your assets at risk.

Case 3: Another example using the same facts with all three children as joint tenants. Your son has three children which you would want taken care of in the event anything ever happened to him. You and your son are out having lunch and are both killed in a car accident. Under the rules for joint tenancy your two daughters will take all the property, essentially eliminating the share that would have gone to your son's three children, your grandchildren.

Only your adult children are joint tenants. Joint tenancy does not provide any protection for their descendents or anyone else that you might want to consider as part of your plan.

Be careful if you anticipate your beneficiaries may be minor children. Many people rely on pay on death clauses and beneficiary designations thinking it avoids probate and other hassles after my death.

While pay on death and beneficiary clauses can be effective for adults, children as beneficiaries can be an issue. Let's say you made your children the beneficiaries of a life insurance policy and they were 5 and 6 years old. Your thinking is, they will have the life insurance money to take care of their living expenses and help the guardian take care of them.

Insurance companies and financial institutions do not like to pay out money to minors. Upon your death the insurance company will either hold the money until your child is 18 or with some additional legal wrangling may pay it out to their guardian. Aside from the fact you may feel 18 is too young to receive a $100,000 life insurance benefit, there is no requirement that they repay money spent by their guardian when they were growing up.

Relying on pay on death and beneficiary clauses can sometimes be more complicated or not result in getting the property to the person you want when they need it.

Organizing your estate under a will or revocable trust allows you to specify directly when and to whom assets are distributed.

In the case of minors or disabled persons, a good will or revocable trust will provide for contingency plans in the event the beneficiary is disabled or a minor. It can also allow your executor or trustee to hold onto the money until they are older or the disability goes away.

If you have a will or revocable trust with a contingent trust or other provisions providing for the minors you can modify the beneficiary clauses in your insurance and retirement accounts to pay to a trustee on their behalf. This allows you to control when your children get full access to the money. It also allows the trustee to provide funds they need growing up to cover education, maintenance and support.

With some contingency planning you protect your children and provide the flexibility to cover their needs without surrendering control to an eighteen year old.

Assets and property with pay on death or specific beneficiary clauses such as life insurance, IRA's 401(k)s and bank accounts will pass to that beneficiary regardless of what your will says.

Thoroughly review and update the beneficiary designations you have made to be sure they continue to reflect your desires and changing circumstances. If your estate is comprised of more that one or two assets or accounts assume the worst and be careful to make sure it doesn't leave anyone out you would want included.

<hr>

Planning Point: Beneficiary Horror Stories, only the names have been changed to protect the innocent. Always check your beneficiaries.

<hr>

Case One - John Brown put his brother on his 401(k) account after his divorce because his children were minors and he knew his brother would take care of them. Years later John dies, his children are all grown and he never went back and changed the designation.

At the time of his death his brother was in a nursing home and incapacitated. John's 401(k) money will go to his brother and his brother's heirs, not John's.

Case Two (Be careful of Separation & Divorce)

Sally and her husband Bill have been separated for 8 years but have never gotten around to getting a divorce. They each have new relationships and separate families they want to take care of. One day Sally dies from an unexpected heart attack. All of her work benefits and insurance go to Bill, who is still her husband.

> *Planning Point: In many states divorce cancels beneficiary designation; however a separation is not divorce so the law will not cancel a designation in that case.*

Consult an estate planning attorney if you have specific desires about how and to whom your estate should be distributed. Make sure you include all of the assets in your planning. Your estate planning attorney can advise you regarding how they will transfer, considering the unexpected.

If you have minor children you will need a will to appoint a guardian. This can only be done through probate after your death. If you have real estate, not all states recognize beneficiary or pay on death deeds. Also the addition of contingency clauses may impact or interfere with clean title to the property.

Use a coordinated strategy of beneficiary designations and pay on death designations to manage the distribution of your estate.

Create a will or living trust which takes into consideration all of your assets and allows you to control the disposition from a single point. If you decide to change how your assets will be distributed you can change it from one document without having to go back to each account or asset.

"You have to admire the Internal Revenue Service. Any organization that makes that much money without advertising – deserves respect. "

Chapter 5 – Understand How Income & Estate Taxes Impact Your Estate

Mistake Number Three: Failing to Plan For Taxes

When you combine estate taxes and income taxes on certain types of inherited property the rates can be as high as 75% - 80%. Just so you know, the courts are looking out for us and have told the IRS it cannot tax at a rate higher than 100%.

There are two kinds of taxes that impact your estate. Income taxes, as most of you are familiar with, and estate and gift taxes. Estate and gift taxes are called transfer taxes and are paid by the person or in most cases that person's estate which is making the transfer. Sales tax for example is a transfer tax. The tax is simple, they add up your total estate when you die, less certain allowable deductions for things like charitable bequests and spousal transfers, apply your estate tax credit and you pay the tax based on what's left.

Your estate for estate tax purposes is everything you own when you die. This includes some items you may not have thought of such as life insurance, IRAs, 401(k)s, even insurance provided through your work.

Life insurance policies can be confusing because they are exempt from income tax but not estate tax. They are included in your estate at face value on the date of your death. This is significantly larger than the cash surrender value the day before you died and can make a big difference in your estate tax calculation. The IRS estimates that is collects 40% of its estate tax from life insurance.

Before you get too concerned, note that the estate tax has historically only been paid by 3% or 4% of the people in the U.S. This occurs for a couple of reasons. One is how the IRS treats a married couple and the second is the IRS gives Americans and resident aliens a credit against the estate tax sufficient to exclude the first $2,000,000 of assets.

The subtle difference between a credit and a deduction is this. The credit is a dollar for dollar reduction of the tax due. The thing to be aware of with a credit is in this case the credit absorbs all of the lower tax brackets and so when the credit runs out each dollar above the covered amount is taxed at a rate of 40+%.

This is different from a tax deduction that is deducted from the taxable amount but leaves the rates the same. A deduction takes dollars off of the top rate by reducing the amount taxable. By providing the benefit in the form of a credit, you may not pay anything, but if you do it will start at a pretty high rate.

In 2007, the marginal rate when the credit is exhausted starts at 41%. This means that if the value of your estate exceeds $2,000,000 everything over that is taxed at 41%. The 41% rate increases from there up to a top rate of 50%. As an example, the tax on an estate of $2,500,000 is $225,000.

The good news is the estate tax credit is increasing to $3,500,000 and then going always completely in 2010. The bad news is unless the law changes the exclusion is going back to $1,000.000 in 2011.

IRS Estate Taxes
2006 - 2011

Taxable Estate	Tax Due 2006- 2008	Tax Due 2009	Tax Due 2010	Tax Due 2011
$ 1,000,000	$ -	$ -	$ -	$ -
$ 1,250,000	$ -	$ -	$ -	$ 102,500
$ 1,500,000	$ -	$ -	$ -	$ 210,000
$ 1,750,000	$ -	$ -	$ -	$ 322,500
$ 2,000,000	$ -	$ -	$ -	$ 435,000
$ 2,500,000	$ 225,000	$ -	$ -	$ 680,000
$ 3,000,000	$ 450,000	$ -	$ -	$ 945,000
$ 3,500,000	$ 690,000	$ -	$ -	$1,200,000
$ 4,000,000	$ 900,000	$ 225,000	$ -	$1,495,000
$ 5,000,000	$ 1,350,000	$ 675,000	$ -	$2,045,000

As you can see the estate tax starts at over 40% -- if you have to pay. It can be even worse if the assets that make up your estate are items like a 401(k) or traditional IRA.

You can get even higher rates if the assets that are being used to pay the tax are coming out of an income taxable asset such as an IRA. Why the increase you ask, because you never paid income tax on these amounts when you were alive, therefore, the tax will be paid by your heirs. The one exception being your spouse, who can roll the amounts over into his or her own account and keep deferring the tax until they collect the money.

Unfortunately, for non-spouse beneficiaries such as children, grandchildren and others, the receipt of your retirement money is taxable and sometimes a double tax impact can occur.

For example let's assume you have an estate of $2.5 million all of which is coming from an IRA. The estate tax is $225,000.

To pay this you need to draw $225,000 out of the IRA to pay the estate tax. When you draw out the $225,000 you will need to pay the income tax on the $225,000. Assuming the tax is 36% you will then pay tax of $81,000 on the IRA withdrawal. Now you need to withdraw another $81,000 to pay the income tax on the $225,000. When you withdraw the $81,000 you will pay income tax on the $81,000 of $29,160. This goes on an on until you finally have paid all the tax on the tax and the tax on the withdrawals. When you are finished the total combined tax exceeds $350,000 on your $2.5 million and that's only if you are lucky enough to live in a state without an income tax. With some planning you could have reduced that tax to $0.00 saving your heirs $350,000.

IRAs, 401(k)s and other deferred compensation plans are valued for estate tax purposes at their full account value. There is no discount because your heirs may have to pay up to 39% in income tax when they get it. Thus, the estate tax will be at full value and you will pay again when the money is received.

To illustrate, your $2,500,000 estate, if comprised of only your IRA and 401(k) balance, your heirs will pay estate taxes of $225,000 on the $500,000 in excess of the $2,000,000 and then will pay income taxes on the whole $2,500,000 as it is distributed over time.

Between the two taxes your key assets could be reduced more than 50%. If you have this type of situation, having a plan could save your estate big time.

There are some strategies to protect yourself and at least make sure you get the full advantage of the credits the IRS gave you.

As I mentioned earlier there is a benefit for married couples. The IRS treats a married couple as a unit for estate and gift tax purposes. This has two planning benefits. First husbands and wives can transfer property back and forth to each other at anytime without any transfer or gift tax. Secondly, assets inherited on your death by your spouse are deductible from your taxable estate.

Thus in the above example if your spouse rolled over the IRA contribution, they would have gotten a deduction for the assets that were transferred to them, reducing your taxable estate to $0.00. The IRS allows you to take this deduction figuring they will still get their share when your spouse passes away. If you have assets that exceed now or could exceed $2,000,000 you need to be aware of how the calculations work and the strategies to avoid it.

Case One: Bill and Mary Jones.

Bill retired with a $2,200,000 401(k) and about $1,000,000 in other assets. Bill passes away and leaves the entire $3,200,000 to his wife Mary.

Mary takes the deduction against Bill's taxable estate for the property transferred to her. By transferring everything to Mary all of it was deducted from Bill's taxable estate value. Thus Bill's estate for tax purposes is $0.00. So instead of paying a tax of $562,500 he pays $0.00.

This sounds good in the short run but when Mary dies two years later she still has an estate of $3,200,000 and does not have a marital deduction. Her only protection is the estate tax credit covering the first $2,000,000. As a result, her estate will pay $562,500 in estate taxes tax on the $1,250,000 which exceeds the $2,000,000, plus whatever growth she experienced in the assets since she received them.

Income Tax Impact: Her heirs will also pay income tax on the $2,250,000 in the 401(k). At a 35% rate the result is a tax of $787,500. A total tax of $1,350,000 or 41.5% of the estate.

If you remember we said each person gets $2,000,000, so why then didn't Bill and Mary have enough to cover the whole $3,250,000 and save $562,500 in taxes?

The point is they each had a $2,000,000 exclusion. However, by using a simple all to my spouse plan, Bill didn't get to use his $2,000,000 exclusion and it cost his heirs $562,500. The $2,000,000 credit is like a coupon is personal to the taxpayer. If you don't use it you lose it.

The point is that between Bill and Mary they could have each used their $2,000,000 coupons and saved $562,500. The question is how do you do this?

One solution would have been having Bills' children inherit the first $2,000,000 using up his credit. But then Mary doesn't have the money and if she needs the money in the future she may not get it back. This is not a good solution for your widow, especially if the assets include the house she is living in and the 401(k) she is living on.

There is a strategy called the by-pass or A/B trust setup which allows a married couple to utilize both credits and shelter $4,000,000 or double whatever the current IRS exclusion is at the time. This strategy is well known but pretty advanced for a do-it-yourselfer because there are different options at different decision points which can have a long term impact.

Planning Point: If you have a large IRA or 401(k) balance you will want to have your spouse as the beneficiary because only spouses can rollover the balances on your death and defer the distributions until they become 70 and 1/2.

This income tax strategy may conflict with you're A/B trust strategy if the IRA or 401(k) is the main asset.

If you have this situation you should probably speak with a professional because there are some special issues you will need to plan around.

If you have a taxable estate or might at the time of your death, you should really seek advice and assistance from an estate planning lawyer. He or she can help you set up a by-pass or A/B trust structure.

The A/B structure allows you to use both exclusions and shelter up to $4,000,000. The good part is it allows the surviving spouse access to the property if he or she needs it to live on.

In simple terms the strategy is to transfer the first $2,000,000, which would be taxable to a trust on the death of the first spouse. The Trust which is considered a different person than the spouse, gets to use the exclusion as the assets, up to $2,000,000 pass through Bill's estate, using up his credit.

The illustration on the opposite page shows the flow of the funds and the result. The exclusion of both spouses is used sheltering the entire $3,250,000 from tax. The survivor maintains control over the assets as trustee. Upon the death of the survivor the funds all flow to the beneficiaries.

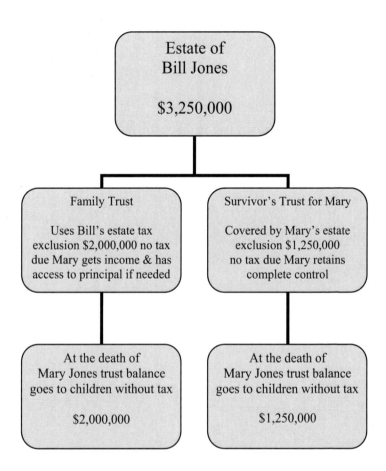

If there are more than $2,000,000 in assets, the excess are transferred to Mary and deducted using the marital deduction. The end result is all of the estate is either sheltered in the Trust or is deducted as it passes to Mary. The beauty of the Trust is the assets are already considered taxed and will grow and eventually pass tax-free to the final beneficiaries. If it grows to a hundred million it will still pass estate tax-free to the heirs. Trusts can be powerful tools if you know how to use them.

The way to prevent taxes from killing your plan is to know when you need to be concerned. If you have significant assets tied up in an IRA or retirement plan you will need to be concerned about income taxes. *(This area is so important we cover it on its own in the next chapter. Mishandle your retirement plans and it could cost your heirs millions.)*

If your estate is approaching the $2 million mark you should probably be doing some kind of estate tax planning. The type of assets that make up the $2 million will influence the type of plan that makes the most sense for you. I would advise against trying to create a proper bypass trust arrangement as a do-it-yourselfer. At the end of the day, the amount of money it would cost to have it done professionally will save you and your heirs significantly in the future. The other benefit is if you mess it up your heirs have no place to seek relief. If your lawyer makes an error they can at least go back against the firm or the lawyer who created the plan.

You can also save some money by shopping around for an attorney that can provide the plan at a competitive price. In every area there is a "going rate" for this type of plan. There are also firms which charge a 30% to 40% premium over the going rate just because they can.

In some ways it is like buying a car from two different types of dealers. One going for volume who deals regularly in the type of car you're interested in and another who is just trying to make the maximum profit they can and figuring that you probably will never be back for any other additional services. If you ask around you can usually find out which ones are which.

Taxes in general are a complex area and the ground is always moving. Every time a new initiative comes along someone has to pay for it.

This someone is always us and the government is always switching methods of charging a tax so no one group gets too upset. It is always a balancing act between cutting certain kinds of taxes and raising others. Basically the philosophy in the area of taxes is to know when you need help. This is your primary concern.

"My father worked for the same firm for 12 years. They fired him and replaced him with a tiny gadget this big. It does everything that my father does, only it does it better. The depressing thing is my mother ran out and bought one."

~~Woody Allen

Chapter 6 – Understanding Your Retirement Plans

Mistake Number 4 – Losing the Big Bucks By Mishandling Your IRA or How to Make a Small Fortune by Starting With a Large One.

A phenomenon has occurred over the last 20 years. The phenomenon is the incredible growth in 401(k) and IRA plans.

Historically, someone retired and received a monthly pension benefit which paid out as long as they lived. When they died it paid their spouse a survivor benefit and when their spouse passed away it just stopped. When you died and this benefit went to your spouse, even though it might represent a valuable asset it was not considered part of your estate. When your spouse died it stopped and therefore it did not create any kind of estate tax problems for you.

Traditional pension plans are on the decline and more employers and individuals are getting pension buyouts or building their nest eggs with tax sheltered 401(k)s and IRAs. Knowing how to manage the distributions can allow you to create a benefit that can go on paying and creating wealth long after your death.

First you have to decide whether you need your IRA or 401(k) money to live on or are to use it as your legacy.

For example, let's say between your savings, Social Security, pension and some annuities you bought when CD rates were at 1%, your retirement expenses are covered.

That means that the funds in your IRA or your 401(k) rollover are not needed for your lifestyle. If this is the case, optimizing the amounts in those vehicles can create quite impressive legacies for your heirs.

Of course, because of certain mandatory distribution rules, you are going to be required to take some distributions during your lifetime.

If you remember our earlier discussion, traditional IRAs and 401(k) plan balances have never paid income tax. Their earnings in the tax deferred protection of your account allow them to grow at a higher rate than they would outside of the plan in your savings account.

It is simple math, if you can grow the assets within your plan at a higher rate than the percentage you are required to withdraw every year your plan will increase in value.

The older you get the more difficult this will become because the percentage you must withdraw increases with your age.

However, if you die with a balance in your account and have your grandchildren as beneficiaries, they could stretch the payout almost forever.

Here is how. Let's assume that at the time of your death you have $100,000 in your IRA account and the beneficiaries on your IRA are your grandchildren ages 12 and 14.

First we'll check out the wrong ways to take the money. They could take the money out in a lump sum. If they do that they would pay all of the tax in one year and the money would leave the tax-deferred shelter of your IRA. Not a great way to build a future.

They can also take the money out over a five-year period spreading the taxes over five years but still losing the tax-shelter of your IRA. Better than a lump sum, but still not a significant source of future wealth.

The best option allows them to withdraw the money from your IRA slowly over their lifetimes.

Remember the simple math, if you earn more in the fund than you remove, the money will continue to increase.

Here is the magic. If they elect to take the money out over their lifetime they will use the same IRS tables you used when you crossed the age of 70 1/2.

These elections do not occur automatically, the beneficiaries have to make this election with the IRA administrator.

They use the same schedule, but will only be 12 and 14. A 12-year-old has a life expectancy under the IRS tables of 70.8 years. This means their required withdrawal would only be 1.4% (100 divided by 70.8) in the first year. Assuming your IRA earned savings account rates of 5%, even after the withdrawal your account will have grown 3.6%.

In year two the mandatory withdrawal only increases a few hundreds of the percentage point.

This means your account compounding with the 3.6% growth from the prior year will grow another 3.6%. Assuming you never do better than savings account rates in your IRA investments your beneficiaries would have to be 63 years old before they would be required to withdraw 5%.

This means that for all the years prior to this your account has continued to build. If you had $100,000 in your account when your 12-year-old granddaughter inherited the fund, not only would she have withdrawn $935,000 but she would still have $1,500,000 million left in the IRA. As you can see the power of compounding in a tax deferred environment creates millionaires.

The numbers also work even without the huge spread in age between a retiree and a grandchild. For example let's assume it goes to one of your own children who is 45 years old. Even at 45 she would only be required to withdraw 2.65% in the first year. Once again, even at savings account rates your fund is building.

The key thing to be aware of when dealing with retirement plans is the ability to stretch the withdrawals out over very long periods of time. Now in some circumstances people don't have the luxury of waiting for their money because of other needs. Also if the accounts are very small, sometimes people take the simple route and just make the distribution.

However if you have a significant balance in an IRA or 401(k) plan some careful planning could make your children and grandchildren millionaires.

If you want to get fancy or exercise more control from the grave you can use a beneficiary trust to control the distributions. It can be set up ahead of time to protect your heirs from themselves and prevent them taking the money in a lump sum. It can also be used as a protection for young children so they do not get control before they have the maturity to handle it.

Asset protection is another factor. A trust composed of inherited assets can be protected from your heirs creditors and still give them significant control of the funds. It creates an intermediary that can manage the flow of funds between the IRA and the beneficiary.

Converting your 401(k) to an IRA is usually recommended once you retire. The main reason is an IRA gives you full control over the investment options on your money and provides additional distribution methods that potentially are not available under your company's 401(k) policy.

For example you could split your IRA into several IRAs, one for each child or one for each grandchild. That way each person could make their own choice about how they withdraw the money. These types of flexible options are not available under a company 401(k) plan.

Or, let's say it is a second marriage for you and your spouse and you both have children from a prior marriage.

You can set aside a portion of you IRA for an individual by using the beneficiary forms correctly.

Another new addition is the ability to make distributions to a charity directly from your IRA without having to withdraw the funds first and then make the contribution out of the funds you received. Even though you were allowed to take a distribution, which was taxable, and allowed a tax deduction for the charitable contribution, the withdrawal would increase your adjusted gross income impacting other deductions and possibly creating limits on your ability to use the full deduction. The direct transfer allows you to avoid the tax on the charitable distribution altogether as the funds go direct to the charity.

There are some other area of IRAs and qualified plans that create special opportunities. If you have a significant IRA there may be some benefits available to lower your tax bill.

If you have company stock in your plan that you have purchased over you're a long period of employment with an employer, things like NUA or Net Unrealized Appreciation on company stock in your plan, can have a significant impact if you have company stock in your plan. You might check with your plan administrator or a financial advisor regarding the benefits available for appreciated company stock.

You should always check your beneficiary forms and the custodial agreement of your IRA administrator to be sure your administrator will allow you to do the things you need to maximize your benefit. If they do not allow certain options you may have to select a new custodian.

"Ordinary people believe only in the possible. Extraordinary people visualize not what is possible or probable, but rather what is impossible. And by visualizing the impossible, they begin to see it as possible."

--Cherie Carter-Scott

Chapter 7 - Taking Care of Your Children & Grandchildren

Mistake Number 5: Knowing How Your Children Will Be Impacted by Your Plan or Why Did They Do This To Us? Fair Doesn't Always Mean Equal.

1. Minor's in Possession

When dealing with children there are several key areas to watch out for. The most obvious is preventing large amounts of cash from ending up in the hands of a 12 year old.

In reality it will more likely be an 18 year old because insurance companies and banks will hold onto funds or require certain safeguards where a minor is the beneficiary. However, once they become an adult at 18 the money will belong to them. If something happens to you there is a good chance that everything you own, plus insurance and 401(k) or IRA benefits will be turned into cash for your heirs. Scary isn't it.

Giving an 18 year old $500,000 in cash may create immediate problems or bad habits or worse. I had a colleague with a client, who on her death left her 18 year old grandson $350,000 cash. The boy had been planning on attending college on a partial scholarship and was going to start in the fall after high school. Upon receipt of the money he decided college could wait and he should see some of the country first. After buying a new car he headed out with his best friend from high school on a cross country trip. The boy returned a little over a year later, broke seeking the shelter of his family. He had fallen in with a hard partying crowd that had gotten him hooked on cocaine and used his money to fund their good times. Once his money was gone, so were his new found friends.

The end result is the money which could have given him a good chance to build his a lifelong dream became his personal nightmare and the wasted legacy of a loving grandmother.

This is not to say that all 18 year olds with money will become drug addicts or use it strictly for the pursuit of short term pleasures. However, they could easily be influenced by friends or family members to use their inheritance to help others or "loan money" for a good cause. If these are not your preferred options on how they should spend your money, maybe you should add some controls.

Parents with young children often think making their children the beneficiaries of their life insurance etc. will allow them to use the money if they pass away. The only flaw in this is if the children are minors the insurance carrier's will not give up the money without a fight and will normally hold the money in an account for the child until they reach 18.

This doesn't give the guardian easy access to the funds and may require some additional legal wrangling to get the child's guardian access to the money. Some form of contingent trust should be available so the minor can get use of the money and have a responsible adult or a professional trust company oversee the management of the assets. These protections can be extended for their lifetime and even passed on to grandchildren if that is something you want. The sophistication of the controls you can put on the funds is limited only by your imagination and the practical limitations of carrying out your wishes. I would caution you that making the restrictions too subjective or attempting to create impossible standards can be a practical problem. For example, say giving them the money when the Trustee thinks they are ready to handle it without any age or other restrictions could create either quick access or no access at all depending on the liberal or conservative nature of the Trustee.

2. Yours, Mine and Ours

Protecting Your Separate Children if You Are not Around.

Finding love a second, third or fourth time around is a wonderful thing and you should protect your new spouse in the event something happens to you. But if you die unexpectedly and your wife or husband finds true love again with someone else, --- your kids may become only a fading memory as your assets go to the heirs of his or her new family. I was an expert witness in one case where the step mother-executor spent $450,000 of the estate's $1,500,000 in assets to fight the deceased's son, who she felt didn't deserve anything. If your not around you won't always know how someone will react in your absence so err on the side of caution.

Only you can gauge the need for this kind of protection, however using a trust to protect the funds for your children in the future while providing your surviving spouse access for his or her needs is a workable solution for everyone involved. As they say, "trust in God but tie up your camels."

If you have significant assets you can establish different types of trusts with different levels of access for your spouse, protecting them against future contingencies, but maintaining your own children as the ultimate beneficiaries of your estate. Other options such as life insurance trusts or splitting your retirement plans can be used to provide a security net for your children.

If you need tax planning or have a very large estate additional trust's known as, Qualified Terminal Interest Property or QTIP Trusts can be used to defer estate taxes while retaining a benefit for your heirs.

Using these types of contingent trusts will require you to employ a professional for assistance. Even lawyers that don't do these kind of trusts everyday will seek professional help from an expert. Getting the language to do what you want and preserving the funds for multiple generations can be tricky.

A man's reach should exceed his grasp, or what's a heaven for.

~~ Robert Browning

3. Inheritance Isn't an Entitlement, Enough Can be Enough.

This is an area where each person has to reach their own decision. You can save your entire life to provide an inheritance for your children so that ultimately they can live better than you did. But is that the point. In today's world, if you have provided your children with the intangibles of a good education, a work ethic and the ability to overcome difficulty by using their own talents and resources, they are already rich. So any money you throw on top of it runs the risk of corrupting this well-balanced person you have already created.

To some people that can sound pretty cold. However, think about it. Unless you are already a member of the idle rich with a trust fund security blanket, your children, productive members of society are going to have to be completely retrained.

The tricky part is you are going to want to retain a certain amount of assets for yourself, because you don't know when you are going to reach the finish line personally and you don't want to run short. Whatever's left over should go to the people you want.

Based purely on my own experience and not on any type of scientific study, 30 years of practicing law and being around new heirs and extremely wealthy people, has taught me that money can be a very corrupting influence. Instead of being an incentive, it can suck the life out of people that had a passion but learn to do nothing because they didn't need to anymore.

In many cases the old adage of the best way to create a small fortune is to start with a large one becomes very true.

Assuming you agree with my philosophy, there are number of ways to achieve this goal and provide support and security for more than just the first generation. Estate plans with fancy names like dynasty trust and generation skipping can provide supplemental income and resources for your children and continue on past their lifetimes to provide similar support for grandchildren and beyond.

Once again these are the type of things that will require some expertise and are not really part of a do-it-yourself program of estate planning someone can download off of the Internet. But if you have the resources and the mental attitude, these very long term types of plans are available.

The main thing in all of these situations is to evaluate who you believe your children are and what you want them to be, and then rely on what you have seen with your own eyes. People do not change as quickly as you might think. If you struggle with them while you are alive, you will probably struggle with them after you are dead.

"A man met a local attorney on the street one day and asked him a business question. He was startled a couple of days later to receive a bill for $150 in the mail from the lawyer.

Not long after that he and the attorney met on the street again.

Attorney: "Good morning."

Man: "Good Morning, but I'm telling you, not asking you."

Chapter 8 – Getting the Best Deal on Legal Fees

Start by Knowing What You Need.

If you turn a bunch of lawyers loose with a budget there are literally thousands of variations in the types of trusts, beneficiary designations and other sophisticated programs they can create for you.

However, at the end of the day the fundamentals of your estate plan will require the following essential documents or their equivalent.

1. **Durable Power of Attorney for Property** - if you become incapacitated, this document allows the person you have appointed to deal with your property and documents on your behalf. This power of attorney deals only with property and does not give you any kind of healthcare decision-making power.

2. **Durable Power of Attorney for Healthcare** -- this document allows you to appoint the person or persons that you want to be making your medical decisions in the event you are unable to make them yourself. This person should be someone who thinks like you do regarding healthcare decisions. This document, while giving someone authority to make your healthcare decisions, does not provide any authority to deal with your property or to sign your name for other purposes.

3. **Living Will or Physician's Directive** -- the living will or physician's directive is instructions regarding how you wish to be treated in the event you have a terminal condition or end up in a vegetative state. Typically these are not overridden by a medical power of attorney

because these are in effect your own desires. And your own written desires will take precedent over what your agent may want.

4. **HIPAA Release** - this is a document that has only become important in the last few years. Under federal law there are certain privacy restrictions on medical information. By preparing a release you are allowing certain people that you have appointed or identified to have access to your medical information. This document does not grant them any power to make medical decisions but only the ability to have access to your information.

5. **Revocable Living Trust** - the revocable living trust has become the workhorse document of estate planning over the last 20 years. It does many things that a durable power of attorney accomplishes and can in many cases do more with your property than a will is allowed to. Used properly, a revocable living trust can allow you to bypass the probate process, handle property in multiple states and deal with tax planning issues all on a completely private basis without the guidance and input of the probate court or other third parties.

6. **Will** - the will is of course the document everyone has heard of. Wills take effect on your death and they do not do anything for you while you are alive. This is the big distinction between them and the documents in numbers 1 through 5. A will is your written instructions to the probate court regarding what you want to happen to those assets which are under their jurisdiction. They do not avoid probate, in fact they require probate to empower them. Understanding the difference as you have seen in Chapter 2 is very important.

In summary, items 1 through 5 all provide benefits for you while you are alive. In combination they are used to provide for contingencies or unexpected situations when you can no longer care for yourself. In those instances where you need to depend on other people these types of documents will allow those that you want to depend on to act on your behalf for your benefit. Items 1 through 4 are typically defined by statute in the state in which you reside. Because they are defined by statute you can often find sample documents either on the Internet or available through your State Bar Association. If you live in less populated states sometimes the availability of these documents can be more limited.

I would also warn you that typically Internet or even state provided form documents can be less flexible and in some cases more limited than documents prepared by an estate planning attorney. So there are some benefits to paying a few hundred dollars to have these done for you

If you require tax planning or are interested in using trust terms or other specialized language to extend your control beyond the grave, I would always recommend you seek a professional. For the same reasons as the paragraph above, mistakes in these more complex areas could be even more costly.

Once you know what you need and the forms you are looking for, you can shop around and ask different law firms what they would charge to prepare the documents you need. You will notice costs will vary tremendously for what are essentially the same documents. My recommendation would be to throw out the most expensive and the least expensive and pick someone priced in the middle. In any case, you should always select someone whose practice is focused in this area. You will also find that price has nothing to do with skill and that some charge more because they can, not because they are worth it.

If you look through the Yellow Pages you will find that just about every attorney in the universe has probate and wills as part of their areas of practice. Attorneys that do not do a lot of estate planning typically prefer wills over a revocable trust because they want you to come back and have to use their services again. In many cases, probate was always seen as the lawyers retirement fund. Write a bunch of wills over the course of your practice and in your later years you can keep busy doing probate work.

I have been party to many conversations among lawyers where pricing had no relation to the work involved but only what they perceived the market would pay. It pays to shop around.

"What you possess in the world will be found at the day of your death to belong to someone else. But what you are, will be yours forever."

Henry Van Dyke
1852-1933

Chapter 9 – Conclusions & Recommendations

The most difficult part of an estate plan is figuring out what you want to happen if you are not around. If you are clear on what you want, the second most difficult job is to select the people you trust and have enough confidence in to execute the plan that you designed.

We hope that reading this short and hopefully interesting book will motivate you to take some steps and design a plan to protect your own estate.

A recap of the basic considerations are:

1. Have a contingency plan in case you are disabled.

    a.   Who will handle my property?
    b.   Who will make my medical decisions?
    c.   Can people take care of me without a guardianship?

2. Understand how the property you own will pass on at your death.

    a.   Probate under my will?
    b.   Under a beneficiary form, joint with right of survivorship or pay on death clause
    c.   Revocable living trust?

3. Understand how income and estate taxes jointly impact on certain assets.

    a.   Is my estate subject to estate tax?
    b.   Have I optimized my estate tax credit?
    c.   Have I protected my heirs from income taxes reducing my estate?

4. Make sure your heirs receive the assets when you want them to receive them.

    a.   Have I protected any minor children or grandchildren?

    b.   Have I protected those who cannot protect themselves?

    c.   Does my plan prevent the wrong people from taking over my estate?

5. Seek professional help if you are uncomfortable doing your own planning.

6. When seeking legal or professional advice find someone you are comfortable with, who can understand your needs. Do not be afraid to shop around. Buying professional services is like anything else, you are the customer, make sure you get what you want.

Even simple steps such as locating your insurance policies, reviewing the beneficiary forms for your employee plans and IRAs and putting in place powers of attorney and other healthcare documents to protect yourself can really help your heirs take care of you and protect your estate.

I thank you for your time in reading this book and hope I have given you a basis for looking at your own situation and putting your affairs in order. Something this important shouldn't be left to chance.

Special Sections Appendix

Those of you looking for additional information the following excerpts from our quarterly newsletter cover some special situations such as vacation homes, retirement plans or family intentions.

You can also visit our website at: www.behlmannlaw.com.

Planning for Vacation Homes, Cabins & Beachhouses

Vacation Home Planning

Some of your family's best memories may be of times spent together at your beachhouse, cabin, farm or other vacation home. Your children may have also used the home during the year to enjoy their own vacations. You may intend for them to continue sharing the property after you pass away. To ensure the "family cabin" is a source of happiness, rather than contention, among your heirs, you should create a plan spelling out the terms of use. The key is to treat the use and ownership of the vacation home as a business. Here are key issues to consider:

Who will own the home?

You might intend to divide ownership equally among your heirs, but if one child lives hundreds or even thousands of miles away and is unlikely to use the home, you may be better off bequeathing him or her other assets. Or, if you decide to give one heir a majority share of ownership, make sure that heir also has a majority share of the financial and maintenance responsibilities.

How will costs be shared?

Ongoing costs can include the mortgage, taxes, insurance, utilities, maintenance, and property management costs if it is also used as a rental. Vacation properties in prime areas have seen tremendous increases in value and their property taxes over the past few years. Maintaining the property can be difficult without sharing the costs among the users.

Who is responsible for cleaning and maintenance?

Financial responsibility is only one consideration; deciding who is responsible for performing the work is another. Cutting grass, paying the light bill, painting and other repairs also need to be handled.

Along with determining overall responsibilities (paying bills, performing routine maintenance, scheduling repairs or renovations, etc.), you should create a list of duties and limitations for family members using the property. i.e. limitations on guests, cleaning up and making sure everything is shutdown or closed up properly.

How can an heir "cash out"?

At some point, one of your heirs may decide they no longer wish to participate in owning the vacation home. Develop a buyout arrangement or exit strategy so an heir can cash out, possibly based on a current property appraisal.

A solid agreement should also specify when each co-owner gets to use the house. You can either stipulate the times yourself or create a rotating "selection schedule" where each heir takes turns choosing the weeks or holidays they are allowed to use the property. Also specify whether your heirs' extended family or friends can use the home. To keep your "family cabin" in the family, make sure it is part of your estate plan.

Treat the creation of the plan like a business and your heirs will be able to enjoy your vacation home as a family, while minimizing discord.

Common IRA Pitfalls

Five Simple Mistakes to Avoid

Common IRA Pitfalls
Five Simple Mistakes You Will Want to Avoid

IRAs are becoming the largest asset in many people's estate. Avoid these common pitfalls to make sure you and your heirs can take advantage of all your hard-earned assets.

Failing to take distributions on time.

You're required to start taking distributions at age 70 ½. Specifically, you must take the distribution for the year in which you turn age 70 ½ (your first year) by April 1st of the year following when you turned 70 ½. If you turn 70 ½ in late 2008, you have until April 1, 2009 to take your first distribution. Since you must take distributions for subsequent years by December 31st of that year you would have to take two distributions in 2009 if you were to wait that long: one covering your first year (by April) and another covering 2009 (by December 31st). A better option may be to take one distribution in 2008 and another in 2009 so you can separate the distributions into two tax years. Either way, if you don't take the required distribution, you'll pay a 50 percent penalty on the amount you should have withdrawn.

Delaying distributions if employed.

If you are still employed, you don't have to take a distribution from your current employer's plan, even if you're 70 ½, but you are required to take distributions from IRAs and 401(k)s from past employers. If you don't, you'll have to pay a penalty.

Failing to designate a beneficiary.

If you die without naming a beneficiary, the IRA's custodial agreement will specify who receives the proceeds. Worse, it may specify that the proceeds be paid out relatively quickly, creating a larger tax burden for the heir. Designate a beneficiary by name, or leave benefits in an IRA Trust so you can control to whom, and how quickly, funds are distributed. Losing the paperwork identifying your beneficiary is also a common problem.

Leaving non-IRA funds to charity.

Charitable organizations do not pay income taxes on qualified IRA distributions, but your heirs will. Leave IRA funds to charity and "non-retirement funds" to your heirs. In many cases, you can minimize or eliminate the tax burden on your heirs through effective estate planning, especially if you bequeath non-IRA or non-401(k) funds.

Tying up assets in illiquid investments.

For example, you may have a portion of your IRA in a Certificate of Deposit. If the face value of the CD is large enough you may have to redeem the CD early in order to take a distribution. As a result, you may have to pay an early withdrawal penalty. Try to avoid tying your money up in CDs, purchase CDs with a relatively low face value, or you can "ladder" the expiration dates to coincide with the required minimum distributions

Family Communications

Family Communications
Best Intentions Contested Outcomes

You may have created the perfect estate plan, but your heirs can easily end up in conflict and your estate in dispute – especially if the provisions of your Trust or Will come as a surprise. Even if your plans are simple, discussing the details of your estate plan with your heirs and family members can help you deal with disagreements or controversies before you pass away.

Communicating your intentions ahead of time is a simple concept, but many people choose not to do so, regardless of the consequences. Studies by the U.S. Trust Company show that less than one-third of persons discuss their estate plans with their children. Over 20 percent of bequest recipients quarrel over inheritance issues. Sixty-three percent of families reporting no disputes over inheritance issues say they had advance notice as to what to expect – and over 80 percent of those families felt they were treated fairly.

If the provisions of your Will or Trust are unusual or differ from state intestacy guidelines, communicating with everyone involved is absolutely critical. If, for instance, you plan to leave 80 percent of your estate to one child instead of splitting it evenly between children, let everyone know the reasoning behind your decision. Simmering resentments can easily boil over into open conflict when a child is surprised by what he or she perceives as unfair treatment. The better your heirs understand your logic, the less likely they are to contest your estate plan. And if there is discord, you are still there to help work your family through any tension.

You can also help reduce conflicts by including a "no contest" clause in your estate plan. In essence, the "no contest" provision translates to, "If you contest this Will or Trust, you forfeit your inheritance." Keep in mind that if you disinherit an heir completely though, the "no contest" clause is ineffective since the heir has nothing to lose by contesting. Also, not every state will honor a "no contest" clause and some states will not honor them if there is any basis for the contest.

Here's the bottom line: make things clear during your lifetime. It's often a mistake to assume everyone will graciously accept your intentions and will "do the right thing." Avoid conflicts after your death that you could have settled during your lifetime, by communicating the plan openly and honestly with your heirs.

Learn What You Need & Avoid Estate Planning Mistakes

This book from nationally known estate planning attorney Richard Behlmann discusses subjects most of us would rather avoid, death, disability and taxes. Many believe that on their death, their family will carry out their wishes and everything will be fine even without a plan of any kind. The truth is that without a plan:

- Your estate could go to the wrong people

- Your children could be without resources

- The government, using your money, will protect your heirs, creating excessive attorney's fees, extra court costs and unnecessary delays in passing on their property;

- You could pay estate taxes and income taxes at combined rates of 75% or more.

This book shows you the problem areas and provides understandable solutions.

- Who will care for me if I am disabled?

- What about probate? Do I need a will?

- How will my heirs pay the taxes on my death?

- What are my estate planning options?

- What if I do nothing? Are you prepared?